BEING YOURSELF

BEING YOURSELF

Margaret Feinberg

Foreword by Luci Swindoll

THOMAS NELSON
Since 1798

NASHVILLE   DALLAS   MEXICO CITY   RIO DE JANEIRO

Published in Nashville, Tennessee, by Thomas Nelson. Thomas Nelson is a registered trademark of Thomas Nelson, Inc.

Scripture quotations are taken from *The Holy Bible*, NEW INTERNATIONAL VERSION®. NIV®. © 1973, 1978, 1984 by International Bible Society. Used by permission of Zondervan. All rights reserved.

Scripture quotations marked NKJV are taken from *The Holy Bible*, The New King James Version (NKJV®). © 1979, 1980, 1982, Thomas Nelson, Inc., Publishers. Used by permission. All rights reserved.

ISBN 978-1-4185-2936-9

Printed in China

12 13 14 15 RRD 10 9 8 7 6

Contents

Contents

Foreword

At the age of sixty-three, the great American poet E.E. Cummings wrote a letter in which he said, "To be nobody but yourself in a world which is doing its best, night and day, to make you everybody else means to fight the hardest battle which any human being can fight; and never stop fighting." I'm not sure of the source of this quote, but I am sure of the truth of it. Being yourself takes stamina, grit, and a great deal of self-assurance.

When I first began speaking publicly, I remember being exceedingly uncomfortable. I was encouraged by a handful of friends who felt I'd do well, but to me it was out of my comfort zone. I was enjoying a career with Mobil Oil Corporation at the time, but to stand up and speak to a crowd was scary and out-of-place for me. I could joke around, be a clown, tell a story . . . but *give a speech?* No way. When I finally gave in to the wooing of God's Spirit and urging of my friends, I devised a little plan I thought would work: *I'll be like my brother, Chuck. He's a wonderful speaker—well loved, totally prepared, and explaining Scripture right and left.* So off I went into the wild, blue yonder trying to be someone I wasn't. I don't know how I thought I'd pull this off because I was neither seminary trained nor as scholarly as my brother, but I gave it a try, thinking it would be easier than being myself. The opposite happened. I was stressed, worn out, and totally uncomfortable!

In a matter of months, the Lord spoke to me in my spirit about my duplicity. He made it clear that He didn't want me to be Chuck. He wanted me to be me! It was as though He said very clearly, *Don't be a teacher, Luci. Tell stories, be a clown, and share your faith in your own way. Just be you. I want you to talk to people like you're visiting with them in your living room.* So before long, I stopped fighting the battle Cummings wrote about, and let go of all that effort to be my brother. I relaxed . . . and public speaking became not only fun but one of the ways God showed me it was okay to be myself.

Sometime later, I told Chuck about this encounter with God and what I thought about it. He said something I'll never forget—"Sis, one of the most liberating things in the world is to know yourself, like yourself, and be yourself. It's life changing." Indeed it is.

Ironically, about a year ago, after I had spoken at a Women of Faith conference, an attendee stopped me on my way out of the arena and said, "Luci, I really enjoyed your message this afternoon. It was very encouraging . . . kind of like you were visiting with me in your living room. I loved that."

Check out this little book and see if you can find yourself between the pages.

—LUCI SWINDOLL

Introduction

Answering One of Life's Toughest Questions

Jesus said to him, "If I will that he remain till I come, what is that to you? You follow Me."

John 21:22, NKJV

Who are you? It's one of the simplest but most difficult questions for anyone to answer. Most people spend their lifetime trying to figure out who they really are. Some of their efforts are healthy and rewarding, but others can be dangerous and even destructive. As a follower of Jesus, you don't have to spend years wondering who you really are! You get to go straight to the source—God—to discover not only *who* you are but who you are created to *be*.

If you wanted to truly understand a painting, who would you ask? The person who purchased the painting? The person who framed the painting? The museum curator? While all those individuals may have insight, the best possible person to ask would be the artist. In the same way, God invites you to understand yourself in the light of who He has created you to be.

Why is it so important to go to God to discover who you really are? Because He's the only one who really knows. He created you. He knows you like no other. You have gifts and talents and desires tucked inside of you that you may not even know about, but God does!

In the following study, you're going to discover who you really are in God's eyes. You're going to learn how simply being yourself sets others free to be themselves. You will have the opportunity to evaluate the unique strengths, gifts, and talents God has given you and how to better use them to serve and love others. And you're going to recognize the rich fruit that grows naturally in your life when you're simply being yourself.

My hope and prayer for you is that through this study you will begin to see yourself as God sees you—beautiful, redeemed, and wonderfully made.

Blessings,
Margaret Feinberg

Just As You Are

God designed you perfectly. You are God's delight, God's handiwork, and you are wonderfully unique. Despite pressures from outside forces that make you feel as if you need to change in order to measure up, God loves you just as you are and more than you could know!

One

You Are God's Delight

The heavens declare the glory of God;
the skies proclaim the work of his hands.

PSALM 19:1

Many voices in our lives try to tell us who we are. Some are well-meaning, including friends and family members. But some of the loudest voices are media. Advertisements and headlines promise better, thinner, stronger, and faster. Rather than tell you who you are, advertisements try to remind you of who you are not and who you could be if you just buy the product.

One of the great secrets of those trying to market a product is simply: *Focus on the benefits, not the features.* This plays into most of the purchases you make whether you realize it or not. If you're buying a computer, a salesperson may tell you it has 16 bytes of RAM. Now if you're not familiar with computers you may wonder, why would I want something to bite my RAM? But if the salesperson told you, this product has 16 bytes of RAM and that means it goes faster and will save you time, now that may pique your interest! Or the salesperson may remind you that buying this particular computer will put you ahead of the game with current technology. After all, this is a computer that will help you learn more and connect more with other people. You won't be the same without it!

When advertisers focus on the benefits instead of the features, *you* take center stage in the sales pitch. You are the most important person, and this product is going to make you even better.

While effective for sales, that approach is a far cry from the one that God uses with us. When He looks at us, He's not concerned with the benefits we can offer Him. He's not asking how we can make Him look better, go faster, or be stronger.

He looks at each of us as inherently valuable, loved, and one-of-a-kind treasures. There's incredible worth just in you! You are a delight to Him. He takes joy in you. And He loves you more than you can ever know. There is not a scale or measuring device that can contain the love God has for you.

The One who fashioned you with great detail and precision loves you beyond measure. Like the Master of all Master Craftsmen, God carefully designed you—each and every one of you—to be a masterpiece.

And that's not a sales pitch, that's a promise you can count on!

1. *Have you ever purchased a product that promised great things but didn't deliver? What was the product? The promise? How did things turn out?*

2. *Advertisers and marketers often try to tell us a lot about what we don't have or what we could be if we purchased their products. Can you think of any other voices in your life that have tried to define you or tell you who you are?*

When it comes to discovering who you really are, only one voice really matters. And God delights over you more than you can you imagine!

3. Read **Psalm 16:3**. How does David view the saints in the land? If David sees people this way, how do you think God sees them?

They are his heroes and they delight in them

The godly people in the Land are my true heroes I take pleasure in them.

God describes His saints as "the glorious ones in whom is all my delight." That means God doesn't just find some of His delight in you—He finds all of it. You are more celebrated than you can possibly imagine.

4. Whether you realize it or not, God has delighted in you before the beginning of time! In Proverbs 8, we get a glimpse of God and His Son, Jesus, at work during creation. Read **Proverbs 8:29–31**. What kind of emotion is expressed in this passage in regard to creation?

happiness & rejoicing

I was there when he set the limits of the seas, so they would not spread beyond their boundaries. And when he marked off the earth's foundations, I was the architect.

5. Why do you think creating the world and mankind was such a delight for God?

I at his side. I was his constant delight, rejoicing always in his presence, and how happy I was with the world he created; how I rejoiced with the human family!

3

6. Why do you think it was such a delight for God to create you?

7. Read **Zephaniah 3:17**. In the space that follows, write out the different things God does in this verse. How have you experienced God doing each of those things in your life?

> *He is a savior.*
> *takes delight in me*
> *Calm your fears*
> *rejoices over me with songs*

The truth is that you are God's delight! You are of infinite worth and loved beyond measure.

8. How does knowing that you're God's delight change the way that you see yourself? Others?

Digging Deeper

Read **Deuteronomy 7:6**. God considers His people His "treasured possession." What possession in the world do you treasure the most? Why is it so important? How much more does God treasure you?

> *For you are a holy people, who belong to the Lord your God. Of all the people on earth the Lord your God has chosen you to be his own special treasure.*

Ponder and Pray

The opening Scripture for this lesson comes from **Psalm 19:1**, "The heavens declare the glory of God; the skies proclaim the work of his hands." If the heavens and skies declare the glory of God, how much more do you? Reflecting on your own life, in what ways does God show His goodness through you? In what ways do you "declare the glory of God" in your decisions, your relationships, and your life?

Bonus Activity

Memorize **Zephaniah 3:17**. You may want to handwrite it on index cards or sticky notes and place them around the house to help you memorize the verse. This week, share with at least one person what this verse means to you.

The Lord your God is with you, he is mighty to save. He will quiet you with his love, He will rejoice over you with singing. NIV

Two

You Are God's Handiwork

And we, who with unveiled faces all reflect the
Lord's glory, are being transformed into his likeness
with ever-increasing glory, which comes from the
Lord, who is the Spirit.

2 CORINTHIANS 3:18

In 1908, Lucy Maud Montgomery published an unforgettable work of fiction about an older couple who adopted an orphan boy but were sent an orphan girl by mistake. The couple decided to keep the child, Anne Shirley, and her adventures of growing up and coming of age launched a best-selling series of books, *Anne of Green Gables*.

There's something lovable about Anne Shirley that generations of readers can relate to and enjoy. Smart, quick, and imaginative, she was eager to please yet took displeasure in her name, freckles, and bright red braids. Throughout the adventures of Anne, we read of a young woman not just coming to terms with life, but with herself and who she's created to be.

In some ways, the story of Anne parallels the story of all of our lives. As we grow older, we are constantly learning new things about ourselves. We discover our likes and dislikes, our passions and joys. We learn about strengths and weaknesses. We learn which things in life come easily and which take lots of work. We discover who we are—and that's not always easy. In fact, in the *Anne of Green Gables* television series, when Anne was asked, "Tell me what you know about yourself," she responded quite memorably: "Well, it really isn't worth telling . . . but if you let me tell you what I imagine about myself you'd find it a lot more interesting."

As a follower of Jesus, you are invited to be your true self—no imagination required! The portrait of who God has made you is intricate, beautiful, and fascinating. You are His handiwork.

Did you know that the Bible says amazing things about you? It says you have been rescued from the dominion of darkness and brought into the kingdom of Christ (Colossians 1:13). The Bible says that you've been anointed, set with His seal of ownership, and given God's Spirit in your heart as a deposit, guaranteeing what is to come (2 Corinthians 1:21–22). And the Bible says that you were chosen by God and appointed to go and bear fruit—fruit that will last (John 15:16).

Indeed, our God has done more than you can ask or imagine. At times, it almost sounds like the fictitious adventures of Anne, but it's wildly true! It's based on the fact of who God is and all that He's done.

God is at work in your life more than you know. That's why one of the most significant callings in your life is to become who you are. By simply being who God has created you to be, you radiate Him. And that's a story that's worth telling.

1. *As a young, feisty woman, Anne took displeasure in her name, freckles, and bright red braids. Are there any things about yourself that you once took displeasure in but which you've learned to appreciate about yourself?*

2. *When you think back on your life, can you isolate a time when you felt as if you came to terms with who you are? What happened? What was the process? What was the result?*

3. *When you think of "Becoming Who You Are," how far along in the process do you think you are on a scale of 1 to 10, 10 being the farthest? Circle the appropriate number.*

1 —— 2 —— 3 —— 4 —— 5 —— 6 —— 7 —— 8 —— 9 —— 10

4. *In what areas are you still struggling to become who you are?*

In opening myself up to others.

5. *In the following chart, draw lines connecting the verses with who you are in Christ:*

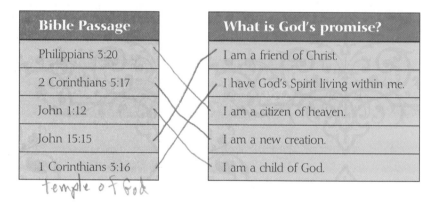

Bible Passage	What is God's promise?
Philippians 3:20	I am a friend of Christ.
2 Corinthians 5:17	I have God's Spirit living within me.
John 1:12	I am a citizen of heaven.
John 15:15	I am a new creation.
1 Corinthians 3:16	I am a child of God.

temple of God

6. *Which of these Scriptures is the most comforting to you? Why? Is there anything stopping you from actually believing these things are true about you?*

Psalm 139 contains a beautiful passage that not only reflects on the intricate detail in which God made each of us, but it also expresses the heart of someone who recognizes that they are God's handiwork. **Psalm 139:13** says, "For you created my inmost being; you knit me together in my mother's womb."

*7. Write **Psalm 139:14** in the space that follows:*

I praise you because I am fearfully and wonderfully made. Your works are wonderful, I know that full well.

Psalm 139:15–16 says, "My frame was not hidden from you when I was made in the secret place. When I was woven together in the depths of the earth, your eyes saw my unformed body. All the days ordained for me were written in your book before one of them came to be."

*Write **Psalm 139:17–18** in the following space:*

How precious to me are your thoughts, O God. How vast is the sum of them. Were I to count them, they would outnumber the grains of sand. When I awake, I am still with you.

In what ways has the psalmist realized that he is God's handiwork? What is the psalmist's response? How does the psalmist's response honor God?

He realized that God is the one who put him together. He praises God for what He has done.

8. *In what areas do you see yourself as God's handiwork? What is stopping you from seeing yourself as God's handiwork?*

The truth is that you are God's handiwork. You are invited to be your true self.

Digging Deeper

As God's handiwork, God goes to great lengths to care for you. Read **Isaiah 46:4**. In what ways is God committed to you? What does God promise to do in this verse? How does this passage make you want to trust God even more?

I will sustain you – I times I will carry you, rescue you even to old age.

Ponder and Pray

The opening Scripture for this lesson comes from **2 Corinthians 3:18**, "And we, who with unveiled faces all reflect the Lord's glory, are being transformed into his likeness with ever-increasing glory, which comes from the Lord, who is the Spirit." This verse is a reminder that you're being transformed. The word in Greek for *transformed* is the same word from which we get the word *metamorphosis*. It's not a one-time event but an ongoing process. In what ways are you being transformed into the likeness of Christ right now?

Bonus Activity

Think about three of your favorite characters from books you've read. What delights you about them? What makes you smile when you think of them? In the same way, imagine God thinking about you. What might come to His mind that brings Him delight and makes Him smile?

Is. 46:4 Even to your old age and gray hairs I am he, I am he who will sustain you I have made you and I will carry you; I will sustain you and I will rescue you.

Three

You Are Wonderfully Unique

When God created man,
he made him in the likeness of God.

GENESIS 5:1

There's no one else like you. You are intricately woven and formed. You have a unique set of talents and gifts, interests and passions. God went to great lengths to make sure you were different from every other human being on the planet. And with more than six billion people, that says a lot!

Just take a moment and look at your fingertips. Notice the intricate detail in those little prints that you see on your fingers. No one else on the entire planet has the exact same ones. In fact, did you know that even identical twins don't have identical fingerprints? If God went into so much detail with your fingerprints, how much more care did He take with other details about you?

Every person has their own traits, personality, and characteristics. Some are inherited from your mother and father and some are influenced by your environment and relationships. Your unique blend makes

15

you one of a kind, part of God's handiwork, and uniquely qualified to help do His work on earth.

Unfortunately, from time to time all of us are tempted to become like someone else—rather than just be ourselves. In an effort to fit in or find acceptance, we may go to all kinds of lengths to pretend we're someone we're really not. We may be tempted to act like we have it all together when we really don't. We may say we love a style or a food that everyone else loves, when in reality it's just not us. Or we may be tempted to buy something we really can't afford in order to "keep up" with those around us. All these efforts rob us of the joy of simply being our true selves.

God wants us to focus on being who He made us to be so we may impact those around us. He invites us to celebrate our uniqueness and be used just as we are. Throughout the Bible, we discover men and women who were uniquely designed to impact lives and change history. We read about a man who lived in the desert and ate locusts and honey to proclaim the coming Savior. We read of a woman who though long past childbearing age was given the opportunity of mother-hood. And we read of a young boy—who in his innocence and gen-erosity—gave a few fish and loaves of bread that were powerfully used to feed thousands.

Many of the men and women throughout Scripture were simply being themselves—their unique selves—and were used mightily by God. Just think of how much God can use you when you're uniquely you!

   1. *Everyone is unique! To discover just how much your personal preferences differ from those around you, respond to each of the following questions, then share your responses with others and see how they differ:*

   What's your favorite store?

What's your favorite hobby?

What's your favorite breed of pet?

What's your favorite flavor of ice cream?

What's your favorite time to wake up in the morning?

2. *Think about your close friends, or even your own family. Does anyone look or act just like each other? What are some specific ways we show our uniqueness?*

3. *Each of us has a unique personality. While numerous books and articles have documented the differences between personalities, many can be identified in four fundamental personality types. Place a star by the two sets of traits that you most recognize in yourself.*

_____ *The Sanguine, or Ms. Popular, is known as the center of attention at a party. She's outgoing, warm, and talkative. She instantly makes you feel at ease and can fill an empty moment with a funny story. She's always ready for the next fun adventure. At the same time, she's quickly distracted, not given to deep reflection, and usually is not the most dependable.*

__√__ *The Choleric, or Ms. Practical, is a hard-working, no-nonsense kind of gal. She's the woman you call when you want to get the job done. She's a natural leader and inspiring to others, but she's often more interested in getting results than in* keeping people happy. If you're in need of a tender moment, she's probably not the best person to call. But if you need to get a project done quickly—albeit not perfectly—she should be the first one you dial.

_¼_ The Melancholy, or Ms. Perfect, is often concerned with style and detail. Introverted, thoughtful, and perhaps artistic, Ms. Perfect doesn't usually act impulsively, but she does feel strongly. She needs to get away from time to time to recharge. When she comes back out, she has meaningful insights into life. While Ms. Perfect has moments of happiness, she also experiences some darker moods and can have difficulty making decisions amid all of her emotions and analysis.

_½_ The Phlegmatic, or Ms. Peaceful, is always a calming presence because she's so laid back. If you're going to lunch, she'll let you pick the restaurant, because she really doesn't care. Her life is lived on Steady Street. Not much gets her up or down—or moving quickly. Rather, she seems to live on cruise control. At times, life happens to her. She doesn't volunteer for a ton of activities, but if you can get her involved, she can be very effective. She's difficult to offend and easy to enjoy, but not the person to call when you need someone to take charge of a situation or confront a problem.

4. Read **Matthew 14:22–28, Matthew 17:1–5,** and **Mark 14:66–72.** In what ways does Peter demonstrate Sanguine personality traits?

He is impulsive
Easily distracted

5. Read *Acts 20:22–24, Acts 20:32–35,* and *2 Timothy 4:7–8.*
In what ways does Paul demonstrate Choleric personality traits?

Once he saw the goal he kept going after it no matter what

6. Read **Genesis 12:1–4, Genesis 13:5–9, Hebrews 11:17–19.**
In what ways does Abraham demonstrate Melancholy personality traits?

He tried to think everything thru. Instead of going alone to Canaan he brought Lot

7. Read **John 11:17–20, John 11:28–33,** and **John 12:1–3.** In what ways does Mary demonstrate Phlegmatic personality traits?

She was content to stay home. She was ready to serve Jesus.

While Peter, Paul, Abraham, and Mary all had different personalities and approaches to life, God used all of them powerfully to build His kingdom and glorify Himself. No matter what personality or blend of personality traits God's given you, He wants to use you! Throughout the Bible, we encounter men and women with unique personalities who were used to do amazing things.

8. Take a moment to reflect on your current relationships—
co-workers, family members, and neighbors. In what unique
relationships has God placed you to encourage and help
someone else? What can you do today to uniquely bless that
person like no one else can?

The truth is that you are wonderfully unique. God celebrates your uniqueness and wants to use you just as you are!

Digging Deeper

In Genesis 1, we read that God made a wide variety of animals and plants. While He was creating living things, He was also busy designing all different sizes, textures, temperatures, and colors. Read **Genesis 1:11–25**. Why do you think God went to such great lengths to provide a variety of creatures on earth? Why do you think He went to such great lengths to make every person unique? How does this passage make you want to celebrate the uniqueness you see in people you know?

Ponder and Pray

The opening Scripture for this lesson comes from **Genesis 5:1**, "When God created man, he made him in the likeness of God." You reflect God—not just in who you are but also in what you share with others about Him. And your story is unique. When was the last time you shared with someone what God has been doing in your life?

Bonus Activity

Read **Hebrews 12:2**. In this verse, Jesus is described as the "author" of our faith. Take a few moments to write a brief summary of the unique story of what God has done in your life. Share it with your friends, family, or study-group members.

The Power
of Being Yourself

*You may not realize it, but there is tremendous power in
simply being yourself. When you are who God created
you to be, then you set others free to be who God created
them to be. The impact is beyond your imagination.*

Four

You Reflect God's Beautiful Design

Grace be with all those who love our Lord Jesus Christ in sincerity.

EPHESIANS 6:24, NKJV

There's a story told of a grandfather who was walking through his yard when he heard his granddaughter repeating the alphabet in a tone of voice that sounded like a prayer. He gently approached his granddaughter and asked, "Whatcha doing?"

The little girl looked up and innocently said, "I'm praying, but I can't think of exactly the right words, so I'm just saying all the letters, and God will put them together for me, because He knows what I'm thinking."

I love that story because it reminds us of the simplicity and beauty of faith. When we don't have the right words or even the letters, God fills in the blanks and puts everything together perfectly—because He knows us so intimately.

As followers of Jesus, we don't just have the opportunity to offer our letters and words up to God in prayer—we get to offer ourselves! Like the story of the young girl, we may find ourselves wondering, *God, what does this spell?* We may not realize that in just being ourselves we are spelling words like *redemption, grace, beauty,* and *hope* to the world around us.

Throughout the Bible, we read of men and women who glorified God with their lives. They spelled out different words and ideas for us by simply being who they were called to be. In studying the life of Abraham we get a living example of faithfulness. David taught us what it looks like to worship. And Ruth gives us insight into loyalty. By simply being themselves, each of these men and women glorified God and left a rich legacy behind them.

At times, all of us may wonder exactly how God wants to use us. If we just offer ourselves to Him, God will take what feels like random letters and spell beautiful words through each of us. Just by being yourself, you reflect God's beautiful design.

1. *Think of a few of the women you know. What are some of the words you see them "spelling" with their lives?*

2. *Think of someone who has recently blessed or encouraged you by simply being him or herself. Describe the experience.*

3. *Throughout the Bible, we read of the different men and women who served God with their lives. They glorified God and were*

used by God by being who they were created to be. Daniel was
forbidden by law to pray or bow to any other god. Read **Daniel
6:6–10**. What words is Daniel "spelling" or demonstrating with
his life in this passage? How does he glorify God?

*Faithfulness
He continued worshipping God even
when he could die for it.*

4. Nehemiah was the cupbearer to the king, but he had a desire
   he could not shake to rebuild the walls around Jerusalem.
   Read **Nehemiah 2:17–20**. What words is Nehemiah
   "spelling" or demonstrating with his life in this passage?
   How does he glorify God?

*Perseverance. He kept on building
even with obstacles in his path*

5. Joseph was sold as a slave to Potiphar, an Egyptian who was
   one of Pharoah's officials. Because of the Lord's favor, Joseph
   quickly found favor with his master. But it wasn't too long
   before Joseph encountered temptation. Read **Genesis 39:1–12**.
   What words is Joseph "spelling" or demonstrating with his life
   in this passage? How does he glorify God?

Purity. work ethic,

6. Lydia was described as a "worshiper of God." She learned about the good news of Jesus and offered a generous response. Read *Acts 16:14–15*. What words is Lydia "spelling" or demonstrating with her life in this passage? How does she glorify God?

She showed hospitality

7. What words do you want God to "spell" with your life?

8. In the following space, write a prayer asking God to use to you to "spell" something beautiful with your life.

The truth is that you inherently glorify God when you are yourself. God wants to spell something beautiful with your life—all you have to do is offer up the letters.

Digging Deeper

In Hebrews 11, we read of the importance of faith. Read **Hebrews 11:1–3**. According to this passage, how would you define *faith*? In what ways is God asking you to trust Him right now? In what ways is God asking you to step out and use your unique gifts to serve others?

Faith is believing God is who He says He is and will do what He says He will do.

Ponder and Pray

The opening Scripture for this lesson comes from **Ephesians 6:24**, "Grace be with all those who love our Lord Jesus Christ in sincerity" (NKJV). This verse is a reminder that grace accompanies as we love God fully. In what ways have you experienced God's grace in your life? In what ways have you had an opportunity to extend God's grace to others?

Bonus Activity

One of the ways we honor and glorify God is through worship. Read **Psalm 100**. Spend a few minutes thanking God for the way He made you! Ask God to continue to use you to bless and encourage others— just by being yourself.

Five

You Will Set Others Free
to Be Themselves

As iron sharpens iron,
so one man sharpens another.

PROVERBS 27:17

Every so often you meet someone who in only a narrow window of time makes an impact on your life. For me, one of those women was Sheila.

I met her years ago after I had just moved into a small home in Pensacola, Florida. She was one of my neighbors, and she was unforgettable! Sheila was feisty and funny. She was strong yet gracious. And a visit with Sheila was nothing less than remarkable. She asked hard questions. She listened patiently. She encouraged firmly. And she loved unconditionally.

Sheila wasn't shy about talking about her own struggles and failures. She was incredibly transparent. Her honesty made me want to be more honest with myself. It wasn't long before her family's home became a revolving door of warmth, grace, and God's love. We shared meals together, watched movies, and talked about life. Whenever I was struggling, I could sit on Sheila's couch and be encouraged by her wise words and prayers. And I wasn't the only one! As her neighbor, I watched as people of all ages flowed through Sheila's front door, spending time on the same well-worn couch enjoying her family and kindness as much as I did.

One day I asked Sheila if she realized the impact she was having on people's lives. She looked at me oddly and said, "What do you mean? I'm a housewife. All I do is cook and clean and care for my family. I hardly leave the house except to shop and go to church."

"Are you kidding?" I asked. "Don't you see how God is using you?" She stared at me blankly.

"Sheila, you've had an incredible impact on my life—all of your encouragement and kindness," I explained. "But there are dozens of others who feel the same way about you. You don't have to leave your house because everyone comes to you!"

That's when she said something I'll never forget: "Well, I'm just being who God made me to be."

I have long since moved away from Florida, but I still keep up with Sheila and she continues to grace me with her wisdom and prayers. By simply being herself, Sheila has blessed countless lives, including my own. She demonstrated a simple but powerful lesson: when you are yourself, you set others free to be themselves. You become a source of encouragement and blessing to others in ways you can't even imagine!

1. *Have you ever had a "Sheila" in your life? Describe the experience.*

2. Have you ever been a "Sheila" to someone else? Describe the experience.

3. Why is transparency so important in a relationship?

Often the people in the Bible and in life whom we most relate to aren't the ones who lived easy, smooth lives, but those who experienced hardship, trials, and even failure. One of the beautiful things about the Scripture is that it tells us the good, the bad, and the ugly of people's lives so they just naturally seem more real and relatable to us.

When we are transparent about our struggles and joys, we express a kind of freedom that's contagious. One of the best scriptural examples of this is the relationship between Elizabeth and Mary.

4. Read **Luke 1:5–7**. What challenge did Elizabeth face?

She was old and childless.

5. In **Luke 1:8–25**, we read a series of miraculous events that Elizabeth and her husband, Zechariah experienced. In the space that follows, make a list of those miraculous events:

*Zechariah offered incense & Gabriel appeared.
Was told they would have a son & gave instructions on how to raise him.
Was struck silent
Elizabeth conceived in her old age.*

6. Meanwhile, Elizabeth's cousin, Mary, was experiencing her own unique series of miraculous events. Read **Luke 1:26–38**. In the space that follows, make a list of the miraculous events encountered by Mary:

*Gabriel appeared to her
Told her she would have a son even though she was a virgin.
The son would be conceived by the Holy Spirit of God & would be the Son of God.*

7. In *Luke 1:39–56*, we discover that Mary went to see Elizabeth and they spent three months together. In what ways do you think Elizabeth was an encouragement to Mary? In what ways do you think Mary was an encouragement to Elizabeth?

They could encourage each other because the both had miraculous pregnancies. Elizabeth, being older probably had some wisdom from her years to share

When we are transparent with one another, we become a source of strength and hope for each other. Through real relationships we can encourage and challenge others to be all that they are meant to be.

8. Looking back on your own life, are there any areas of struggle that you've faced where you can now become a source of encouragement for others? Who is God calling you to help set free by simply being yourself and loving unconditionally?

The truth is that when you are yourself, you set others free to be themselves. You become a source of encouragement and blessing to others in ways you can't even imagine!

Digging Deeper

Jonathan and David had an amazing friendship in which both men were encouraged to be themselves. Read **1 Samuel 18:1**. Which relationship in your life has most been like a Jonathan/David relationship? When was the last time you connected with that person? Prayed for that person? Encouraged that person?

Ponder and Pray

The opening Scripture for this lesson comes from **Proverbs 27:17**, "As iron sharpens iron, so one man sharpens another." This verse is a reminder that we are called to encourage and challenge one another. Who in your life challenges you to grow in your relationship with God and love Him more fully? Who are you encouraging and challenging to grow in their relationship with God right now?

Bonus Activity

Make a list of three people who have been like a "Sheila" to you by encouraging and inspiring you. Write them a card, letter, or e-mail letting each person know the impact they've had on your life and how grateful you are for them.

Six

You Help Fulfill
God's Greater Purpose

For even the Son of Man did not come to be served,
but to serve, and to give his life as a ransom for many.

MARK 10:45

Clara Frasher watched as students poured into the high school across the street from her home in Gainesville, Texas. She felt a burden on her heart that she just couldn't shake. She didn't know what she could do to reach the teens, so she began praying. She even invited some women she knew to meet once a week to pray specifically for the students who attended the school. Those prayer meetings lasted six years.

After a few years, a youth minister by the name of Jim Rayburn moved to the area and accepted a position working with youth at a local church. The youth meetings—which reached many unchurched kids— were well-attended and popular in the community. Eventually, Rayburn felt led to start his own organization. Since then, Young Life has grown into an international organization that reaches one million teenagers annually through its ministry. Even to this day, the organization attributes much of its initial success to the faithful prayers of those women.

Clara felt a unique burden on her heart, and in response she prayed and God faithfully answered. Like Clara, you have a unique role to play in changing the world around you. God has uniquely wired you to be attentive to particular issues, needs, and people. And when you respond, God can use you to fulfill His greater purpose of redeeming people and bringing them back into a closer relationship with Himself.

Each of us has a unique role to play that makes a difference in the world around us. It's like a symphony. Without every member playing their instrument at the right time, the music doesn't sound as good as it could. In the same way, each of us has a role to play—including you! As the Great Conductor, God invites us to fix our eyes on Him: to play the song that we have been called and created to play since the beginning of time.

Throughout the Bible we read of men and women who were used mightily by God by simply using the talents and gifts they had been given. No matter what your age or stage of life, you're invited to be part of God's symphony and reveal God's goodness to the world around you. Like Clara and the women she faithfully prayed with, there's no telling what God might do through you!

1. *What kinds of issues, situations, or people tend to burden your heart?*

2. *Why do you think God uniquely wired you to be sensitive to these burdens?*

3. How have you responded to these burdens?

Daniel was a man who was used powerfully by God by simply being himself and being faithful to the gifts he had been given and the burdens placed on his heart.

*4. Read **Daniel 1:1–21**. In this passage, what gifts and talents are given to Daniel according to Daniel 1:4, 17?*

Strong, healthy, good looking, well educated, good judgement. ability to understand every aspect of literature & wisdom. interpret meaning of visions & dreams

5. What burden did Daniel feel on his heart (v. 8)? What was the result of being faithful to that burden (v. 15)?

Not to defile himself by eating the food & wine from the kings table.

Daniel was given a unique gift of dream interpretation. It wasn't too long until Daniel had the opportunity to use his gift not only to save his own life but the lives of his friends. King Nebuchadnezzar had a dream that troubled him. When his counselors could not tell him the dream, he threatened to have all the wise men of Babylon put to death.

6. Read **Daniel 2:14–23**. How did Daniel respond to the news? What did Daniel ask his friends to do?

He went to the king and asked for more time. He asked his friends to pray that God would show them the secret.

7. Read **Daniel 2:26–49**. What was King Nebuchadnezzer's response to the dream interpretation (vv. 46–49)?

He fell down & worshipped Daniel & God. He ordered the people to worship them. He placed Daniel as ruler over Bobylon

> The truth is, everyone has a role to play in making an impact on the world around them. When we offer ourselves—our whole selves—to God, He can use us in ways we can't even imagine!

Daniel was uniquely used by God. He had a rather unusual gift—dream interpretation— but still used it not only to save himself and his friends, but the king and the kingdom. In fact, the impact of his gift is still being felt today as we read of his unique prophecies in the Bible.

8. *Do you think Daniel ever knew the full impact he had on his king,*
   kingdom, and history? Do you think anyone—including you—can
   ever know the full impact we have by simply being ourselves and
   responding to the needs of our world? Why or why not?

Probably not completely because
his influence is still being felt today.
He probably saw a little in his
lifetime.

Digging Deeper

The gifts we're given can be used for many purposes. What is the real
purpose of the unique gifts you've been given? Read **1 Peter 4:10–11**.
Think of the specific gifts you've been blessed with. How can you use
your gifts to honor God? Is there anything you need to change in your
attitude or the application of your gifts?

Gifts are to be used to serve others
and bring glory to God.

Ponder and Pray

The opening Scripture for this lesson comes from **Mark 10:45**, "For
even the Son of Man did not come to be served, but to serve, and to
give his life as a ransom for many." This verse is a reminder that one of
the purposes of our lives is to serve others. In what ways are you serving others right now? In what ways are you giving your life for others?

Bonus Activity

Make a list of the people who have had a real impact on your life over the years. How many of them realized the impact that they had? Spend some time praying for each person. Ask God to bring people into their lives to bless them, as well.

Knowing Yourself

You already understand the importance of being yourself.
But part of being yourself means knowing yourself—your
strengths and gifts as well as your weaknesses—so that
you can be all that God created you to be.

Seven

Aware of Your Triggers

No temptation has seized you except
what is common to man.
And God is faithful; he will not let you be tempted
beyond what you can bear.
But when you are tempted,
he will also provide a way out
so that you can stand up under it.

1 CORINTHIANS 10:13

A few years ago, someone asked me a question I'll never forget:

Is there a trigger in your life that causes you to sin?

I had never thought about that question before. I was well-versed in listing my areas of weakness and temptation—a rather ugly list that included things like pride, anger, gluttony, slander, and selfishness. I live in a fallen world where sometimes the things I really don't want to do get the best of me. I am grateful for God's forgiveness and grace, but I had never thought about what really brings those issues—those sins—to the surface.

As I thought and prayed about the question, I realized that the thing that causes me to sin most often was rather simple and obvious: lack of sleep. When I don't get a good night's rest, I tend to be short with people and less forgiving. I'm more critical and selfish. I feel cranky, and rather than think on those things that are good and true and beautiful, I find myself distracted by anything uncomfortable or negative. I also tend to overeat for energy boosts throughout the day.

Once I recognized that lack of sleep was a trigger point for sin in my life, I began to pray that God would use this realization to transform me. Since then, I've learned to value a good night's sleep much more. When I'm well rested I'm better equipped to handle the curve balls of life that are thrown my way; and with God's help, I'm finding myself better equipped to respond in kindness and love rather than anger and pride.

When you allow yourself to be who you are, you are naturally vulnerable to a particular set of temptations—and triggers that ignite those temptations—that are specific to you. This is one reason that knowing yourself is so important. By being aware of the triggers that can cause us to give in to sin, we can learn to guard ourselves from sin and focus our time and energy on our God-given strengths.

1. To what areas of sin are you particularly prone?

2. Is there a trigger in your life that causes you to sin?

3. *What steps can you take to remove the trigger that causes you to sin?*

Samson was one of the great judges in the Old Testament. He was separated to be a leader as a Nazirite, which required him to follow specific guidelines for his life. He was a man of great physical strength, yet he was weak when it came to resisting temptation.

4. *Read **Judges 16:1–4**. According to this passage, what was one of Samson's great weaknesses? What would you say was his "trigger"?* women, lust

5. *Read **Judges 16:5–14**. How did Samson respond to this area of weakness in his life? Would you describe his actions as running away from his weakness, resisting his weakness, or* <u>*flirting with his weakness?*</u> gave in to it

6. *Read **Judges 16:15–21**. According to this passage, what caused Samson to give in to his weakness (v. 16)? How could Samson have avoided giving in to his weakness?* Deliah kept nagging him and he gave in.

7. What effect did Samson's giving in to sin have on him being all that God had designed him to be? *He was enslaved. Bound, blinded and imprisoned*

8. Why do you think it's important to be aware of your "triggers"? *So you are more able to avoid the temptation.*

The truth is that by being aware of your weaknesses and the triggers that cause you to sin, you can learn to guard yourself from sin and focus your time and energy on your strengths.

Digging Deeper

Sin is powerful, but God is even more powerful. Read **Romans 6:20–23**. In what areas of your life have you felt as if sin has controlled you? In what areas of your life have you felt like you've overcome sin through God's strength?

Ponder and Pray

The opening Scripture for this lesson comes from **1 Corinthians 10:13**, "No temptation has seized you except what is common to man. And

God is faithful; he will not let you be tempted beyond what you can bear. But when you are tempted, he will also provide a way out so that you can stand up under it." This verse is a reminder that you will never be tempted beyond what you can handle. When you face temptation, what is the most common "way out" that God provides for you to escape? Does anything hinder you from taking the "way out"?

Bonus Activity

Spend some time asking God to reveal areas of temptation and weakness in your life. Now ask God to reveal the way out in each situation. Is there anything that you need to change in your schedule, activities, or relationships in order to avoid temptation? If so, take the steps needed to make a change.

Eight

Playing to Your Strengths

*So I was afraid and went out and
hid your talent in the ground.
See, here is what belongs to you.*

MATTHEW 25:25

Think about a student who comes home with a report card. Reading down the list of grades, every single subject gets an A—except one, which gets a C. Now which grade on the report card will probably get the most attention? In many homes it's the subject that gets the lowest score.

Most of us are far more aware of what we're not so good at than our real gifting, talents, and skills. We have a natural tendency to focus on improving the C subjects rather than play to our strengths. While it's important to be aware of our weaknesses and any areas where we're prone to temptation (as discussed in the previous lesson), we are also called by God to use the talents and gifts that we've been given to serve others. If we focus all our attention on our weaknesses, then we inadvertently bury our talents.

God invites us to discover the talents and gifts that He has given us and use them to honor Him and serve others. Throughout the Bible, we read of men and women who played to their strengths. David was gifted with music and writing lyrics. Because he poured time and energy into this natural gifting, we get to enjoy an amazing book in the Bible: Psalms. Solomon was given wisdom beyond measure, and he was able to use that wisdom to extend justice to his kingdom. Anna was given a gift of prophecy. She played to her strength by spending her life in the temple praying, serving, and waiting for the promised Savior. Once she encountered Jesus, she continued to tell others about Him.

Every person has a unique blend of experiences, talents, and gifts that are meant to be used to honor God and serve others. When you focus on these areas, then you begin playing to your strengths. The impact will be unimaginable!

1. How would you describe yourself? What comes to mind?

Generally, we are far more aware of our weaknesses than our strengths. As a result, we ~~can~~ spend more energy focusing on what we're not as good at rather than on the gifts and talents that we've been given.

2. Why do think people naturally have a tendency to focus on their weaknesses rather than their strengths?

It is often thought that that would be pride.

3. How much attention do you give to your weaknesses compared to your strengths?

Everyone has a unique blend of talents and strengths. As we use our talents and strengths as followers of Jesus, we become like a body—many parts working together. One of the places in the Bible where this is demonstrated was in the construction of the tabernacle. Through the generosity of the people and the talents of specific individuals, the tabernacle was built. Read **Exodus 35:20–35**.

4. What specific talent was given to Bezalel by God? Why was this particular talent so important in the construction of the tabernacle? He was a master craftsman skilled at working with gold, silver, bronze, engraving, mounting gems, and carving wood. Also able to teach these skills to others.

*5. Read **Romans 12:3–8**. Why do you think God gives people different gifts and talents?* So that working together His Word will advance and His work will get done.

6. Have you ever tried to do something outside of your gifting? What was your experience? What was the result?

7. Think of someone within your church or community who is really making an impact. In what ways are they playing to their strengths? What is the result?

8. Are there any areas in which God is calling you to play to your strengths? What steps do you need to make to play to your strengths?

The truth is that every person has a unique blend of experiences, talents, and gifts that are meant to be used to honor God and serve others. When you focus on these areas, then you begin playing to your strengths. The impact will be unimaginable!

Digging Deeper

Sometimes it's easy to be distracted by our inadequacies, but the Bible reminds us that our strength is found in God. He is the One who is working within us. Read **Ephesians 3:20–21**. What hope does this passage give you regarding God's work in your life? What hope does this passage give you regarding God's desire to use you?

God is able to do more in & thru us than we could imagine. I need to become willing to let God mold & make me.

Ponder and Pray

The opening Scripture for this lesson comes from **Matthew 25:25**, "So I was afraid and went out and hid your talent in the ground. See, here is what belongs to you." This verse is part of a larger story about three men who were given talents. Two multiplied their talents and one buried it. Read **Matthew 25:14–46**. In what ways are you using the talents God has given you? Do you have any buried talents in your life? What steps do you need to take to unearth them and begin using them to honor God and serve others?

Bonus Activity

On a blank piece of paper, write out your general schedule for the week. What do you do each day? Spend some time prayerfully reviewing your calendar. How much time each week are you spending playing to your strengths? Are there any activities you need to cut out of your schedule so you can begin using the gifts and talents God has given you?

Nine

Your Greatest Strength,
Your Greatest Weakness

But I have prayed for you, Simon,
that your faith may not fail.
And when you have turned back,
strengthen your brothers.

LUKE 22:32

Did you realize that your greatest strength is linked to your greatest weakness? When we think about strengths and weaknesses, most of the time we think of them as being in different categories, but the truth is that they're often related.

For example, extroverts usually get their energy from being with other people, whereas introverts usually get their energy from being alone. Being either an extrovert or an introvert has its own strengths, but also has its own weaknesses. An extrovert may not be comfortable with silence or being alone, whereas an introvert may feel exhausted or even uncomfortable around lots of people.

If one of your strengths is getting things done and being productive, then you may be tempted to prioritize projects over people. If one of your strengths is being laid back and relaxed, then time management may be an area of struggle. If one of your strengths is seeing the big picture, then the details of an event may be difficult to manage. If one of your strengths is attention to detail, then keeping your eyes on the big picture may be challenging.

In other words, being good at one thing means you're probably not going to be good at something else. The beauty of recognizing that your strengths and weaknesses are linked together is that you can develop compassion and grace not only for yourself, but for others, as well. We are then free to recognize that we don't have to be all things to all people and we can develop healthy expectations in our relationships.

1. Make a list of your greatest strengths. Do you recognize any weaknesses that are linked to your strengths?

2. How does recognizing that your strengths and weaknesses are linked help you have more grace for yourself? For others?

3. Review the following list of adjectives. Circle the ones that best describe you.

Researcher	(Artsy)	Recruiter	(Teacher)	Promoter
(Analytical)	Creative	Manager	Writer	Relational
(Mathematical)	Colorful	Interviewer	(Reader)	Talkative
(Organized)	Designer	(Planner)	(Editor)	Connector

Do you see a common link or pattern between the items for which you're naturally gifted?

In **Luke 10,** we read the story of Mary and Martha, two godly women with very different strengths, weaknesses, and personalities.

*4. Read **Luke 10:38–40.** What strength of Martha's is displayed in these verses? What strength of Mary's is displayed in these verses? What weakness of Martha's is displayed in these verses? What weakness of Mary's is displayed in these verses?*

Martha: She is organized, managing servants to get things done. She was hospitable.

Mary was spending time with Jesus - their guest

Martha wasn't paying attention to Jesus.

Mary wasn't concerned with any of the preparations to serve Jesus.

61

5. Read *Luke 10:41–42*. *How did Jesus respond to Martha and Mary? What does this passage reveal about the tension that can arise between our strengths and weaknesses?*

He calmed them both.

When we place ourselves in different situations, our strengths and weaknesses reveal themselves in different ways. In John 11, we discover that Martha was a woman of great strength and faith while Mary stayed home during the arrival of Jesus.

6. Read *John 11:17–32*. *What strengths are displayed by Martha in this passage? What weaknesses are displayed by Martha in this passage?*

Her faith was strong. She knew if Jesus had been there her brother wouldn't have died. She believed in the resurrection.

7. *What strengths are displayed by Mary in this passage? What weaknesses are displayed by Mary in this passage?*

She too believed Jesus. She fell at His feet weeping.

God makes each of us unique. God weaves us together with different strengths as well as inherent weaknesses. Yet He can use all of us to bring honor to His name.

8. *Are there any areas of weakness in which you've been too hard on yourself or someone else? Are there any areas of strength you have been hesitant to celebrate in your own life or in the life of someone you know?*

Digging Deeper

Sometimes it's easier to recognize someone's weaknesses rather than their strengths. But when we choose to focus on a person's strengths, then we become cheerleaders and supporters of not only that person but also what God is doing in their life. Read **Philippians 2:19–24**. In what ways is Paul being an encouragement to Timothy in this passage? How can you become an encourager to those around you?

He complimented him on the things he did and was going to entrust his ministry to the Phillipians to Timothy by sending him there.

> The truth is that our strengths and weaknesses are often linked. No one can be great at everything. That's why recognizing the link between strengths and weaknesses can help you develop compassion and grace not only for yourself but others.

Ponder and Pray

The opening Scripture for this lesson comes from **Luke 22:32**, "But I have prayed for you, Simon, that your faith may not fail. And when you have turned back, strengthen your brothers." Read **Luke 22:31–34, 54–62**. How are Simon Peter's greatest strengths and weaknesses displayed in this passage? What encouragement does Jesus offer Simon Peter? What encouragement do you find in this passage regarding your own weaknesses and failures?

Bonus Activity

Think of at least one person in your life with whom you tend to recognize a weakness. Spend some time praying for this person. Ask God to reveal the strength that's inherently linked to this weakness. If you get the chance, look for an opportunity to encourage the person this week and recognize the natural gifts and talents God has given the person.

The Fruit
of Being Yourself

When you are simply being who God created you to be,

you can't help but live a fruitful life. People will love

seeing God's radiance in you.

Ten

Developing God–Esteem

For in Him we live and move and have our being,
as also some of your own poets have said,
"For we are also His offspring."

ACTS 17:28, NKJV

There's a story told of a fifth grader who came home from school with a huge smile on her face. She had just been voted, "The Prettiest Girl in the Class." The next day she came home bubbling with excitement. She had just been voted, "The Most Popular Person in the Class." A few days later, the young girl won a third contest, but she didn't say anything about it to her parents. When her mother noticed the girl's unusual silence, she asked, "What were you voted this time?"

The young girl looked down at the ground and whispered, "The Most Stuck-Up Person in Class."

At times, all of us get a little stuck on ourselves. Whenever we find our self-worth in the approval of others, sooner or later we're going to be disappointed, like the young girl was. When we find our value in what others think of us, then we're more likely to give in to pride and even arrogance. The truth is, all of us have tremendous worth, but our value is not in what others think, but in what God thinks!

God is our true source of confidence, faith, hope, peace, love, and joy—everything that we hope to be and are meant to be. When we begin to find our value and worth in Christ, then we begin building our lives on a rock-solid foundation. We are no longer subject to the shifting sands of other people's opinions. And in the process, we begin to develop God-esteem rather than self-esteem.

God-esteem fills us with the confidence that no matter what happens, we are loved and treasured by God. We can believe that God has our best interests in mind and He sees the things that truly matter. He recognizes the beauty within us that we cannot see ourselves. When we keep our eyes on God, then we begin living for an audience of One and find ourselves more free than ever to simply be ourselves.

1. *Which do you think is better: God-esteem or self-esteem? Why?*

It isn't going to change.

2. *Are there any areas in your life where you're particularly susceptible to finding your value or worth in something other than God?*

3. *In your own life, what does it mean to you to live for an "audience of One"?*

4. *According to the following verses, why should we find our value and worth in God?*

1 Samuel 15:29: *It isn't going to change and is the truth*

Psalm 119:89–90: *It is eternal*

Isaiah 46:4: *God will keep us, carry us, and rescue us all our life*

Isaiah 54:10: *His love will never be shaken,* a compassion *or removed.*

In the Sermon on the Mount, Jesus advises the following in **Matthew 6:19–21**, "Do not store up for yourselves treasures on earth, where moth and rust destroy, and where thieves break in and steal. But store up for yourselves treasures in heaven, where moth and rust do not destroy, and where thieves do not break in and steal. For where your treasure is, there your heart will be also."

5. *While this passage clearly addresses financial and material goods, what non-material "treasures" are you tempted to try to store up on earth? What non-material treasures should you want to store up in heaven?*

6. What does it mean to you when Jesus says, "Where your treasure is, there your heart will be also"?

Your actions will go to what you treasure. You will protect that.

7. Where is your treasure right now? Where are you investing your energy, your value, and your worth?

8. Are there any areas where God is calling you to live for an "audience of One" right now?

Digging Deeper

The foundation from where we get our value and worth is extremely important. If our value and worth come from others, then we will be tempted to listen to their voices rather than God's voice. Read **Matthew 7:24–27**. Why is listening to God's voice and finding our value in what He says so important? Have you ever experienced a storm of life when you felt like your home crumbled? Have you ever experienced a life storm when you felt like your home stood strong?

That is what will last. It is a strong foundation on which we can build our life.

Ponder and Pray

The opening Scripture for this lesson comes from **Acts 17:28**, "For in Him we live and move and have our being, as also some of your own poets have said, 'for we are also His offspring'" (NKJV). In what ways do you feel like you live and move and have your being in God? In what ways do you recognize yourself as God's offspring?

> *The truth is, all of us have tremendous worth, but our value is not in what others think, but in what God thinks. God invites us to find our esteem in Him and live our lives for an audience of One.*

Bonus Activity

During the upcoming week, set aside a special portion of time to spend with God one-on-one. Imagine yourself before God and He is your "audience of One." Talk to God honestly, vulnerably, and freely. Ask God a simple but powerful question, "What do you think of me?" Then spend time listening. Keep a Bible nearby and enjoy the time in simply being with Him.

Eleven

Radiating the Joy–Filled Life

For the joy of the Lord is your strength.

Nehemiah 8:10

Did you know that doctors have discovered something that can help relieve stress and even alleviate hypertension? It doesn't require eliminating bacon and ice cream, going to the gym, or taking a prescription. What is the activity? Laughter!

The medical community has discovered that laughter really is the best medicine. Hearty laughter is known to reduce blood pressure and heart rates. In fact, a recent study found that those with heart problems were 40 percent less likely to respond with laughter to day-to-day situations. In other words, laughter doesn't just doesn't make you feel good, it actually contributes to your overall health and well-being.

While happiness is based on outward circumstances, joy is dependent on our inward character. You can't help but encounter joy when you encounter Jesus and all that God has for you and has created you to be.

Joy naturally bubbles up when you begin expressing gratitude for what you have rather than focusing your attention on areas of lack. Joy stirs in your heart when you focus on others and invest in something bigger than yourself. Joy is unavoidable.

The source of real joy is Jesus. As you grow in your relationship with God, one of the natural fruits that grows is joy. It's not something you have to force or manufacture. It literally springs up inside you. Joy is also contagious. Not only will joy shape your attitude and encounters with others, but it draws other people to you. Joy is like a magnet—everyone wants to be around someone who is joyful.

1. *What do you think are some of the differences between happiness and joy?*

   Joy is lasting happiness temporary

2. *At what points in your life have you felt the most joy? Describe them in the space that follows. Do you see any common themes in those moments?*

3. *Are there any things that tend to steal your joy or prevent you from embracing a joy-filled life?*

Jesus is the ultimate source of joy in our lives. After Jesus died on the cross, we read that He appeared to his disciples several times.

4. Read **John 16:22.** *What does Jesus promise regarding the joy the disciples will experience?* No one can take it away

5. Read **John 20:19–20.** *When did the disciples experience gladness and joy? What was the cause?*

When they saw Jesus after he had risen.

The joy that God offers us is much different from temporary happiness or fleeting pleasure. It is lasting, and it springs out of who God is.

6. Read **Psalm 16:11.** *According to this passage, what kind of joy does God offer us? He offers us the joy of His presence, and He offers us eternal pleasures—joy that lasts forever.*

full joy

One of the ways that we can experience joy is through worship. As we worship God, joy comes alive in our hearts.

7. *Look up the following Scriptures and write out the following verses:*

Psalm 33:21: *For our heart is glad in him, because we trust his holy name.*

Psalm 63:5: *My soul will be satisfied as with fat & rich foods and my mouth will praise you with joyful lips.*

Psalm 64:10: *Let the righteous one rejoice in the Lord and take refuge in him. Let all the upright in heart exalt!*

Psalm 97:12: *Rejoice in the Lord O you righteous and give thanks to his holy name.*

8. *Is there anything preventing God's joy from abounding in your heart?*

> *The truth is that you are designed to radiate God's joy. As you grow in your relationship with God and worship, you can't help but radiate joy.*

Digging Deeper

The joy that God gives us is almost beyond description. It's different than happiness. Read **1 Peter 1:8**. How would you describe the joy that you've experienced from God? What adjectives would you use? What do you imagine the joy we'll experience in heaven will be like?

inexpressible

Ponder and Pray

The opening Scripture for this lesson comes from **Nehemiah 8:10**, "For the joy of the LORD is your strength." In what ways does joy give you strength? In what ways does joy give you the strength to strengthen others?

Bonus Activity

Think of someone you know in your life whom you would describe as joyful. During the upcoming week, schedule a time to get together or talk on the phone. Let the person know how much you appreciate their joy and ask the person, "What's the secret of your joy?" You just might be surprised what you discover!

Twelve

Loving Others Unconditionally

The LORD appeared to us in the past, saying:
"I have loved you with an everlasting love;
I have drawn you with loving-kindness."

JEREMIAH 31:3

A story is told of a wealthy plantation owner who had several slaves. One day, the plantation owner discovered one of his slaves reading his Bible. The plantation owner was angered and scolded the slave for neglecting his duties. After all, Sunday provided more than enough time to study the Scripture. To make a point, the master had the slave whipped and locked up in a shed.

A few hours later, the slave owner walked by the shed. He could hear the voice of the beaten slave. He leaned his ear next to the shed wall and discovered the slave praying and asking God to forgive the unfair and unjust actions of the slave owner. Then, the slave prayed that his owner would have his heart touched by God and become a good Christian.

The slave owner walked away from the shed, but he couldn't shake the weight of the slave's words on his soul. Eventually he turned to

God and became a follower of Christ. Through the slave's prayer of hope and love, his master's life was changed forever.

It's impossible to measure the full impact of love. When given unconditionally, love has tremendous power not only to transform the person we choose to love but also ourselves. Nowhere is that demonstrated more clearly than in Jesus who freely gave up His own life so that we may experience saving grace and a relationship with God.

When we are truly being ourselves and loving ourselves as God designed us to be, then we are better able to love others. As we come to terms with who we are—imperfections and all—then we are better able to love others with their imperfections. That's why the law of love is the most important law of all. It is a transforming power not only in our own lives but also in the lives of countless others.

1. *Can you think of a time in your life when you felt loved unconditionally? How did it impact you? How did the experience encourage you to become who you truly are?*

2. *Can you think of a time in your life when you were committed to loving someone unconditionally?*

Paul was known for his incredible words of wisdom and instruction in the New Testament. In **Ephesians 3:14–19**, we read of one of his most profound prayers, "For this reason I kneel before the Father, from whom his whole family in heaven and on earth derives its name. I pray that out of his glorious riches he may strengthen you with power through his Spirit in your inner being, so that Christ may dwell in your hearts through faith. And I pray that you, being rooted and established in love, may have power, together with all the saints, to grasp how wide and long and high and deep is the love of Christ, and to know this love that surpasses knowledge—that you may be filled to the measure of all the fullness of God."

3. Read **John 15:12**. *According to this passage, what is the distinguishing mark of being a follower of Jesus?*

By our love for one another

4. *Why do you think it's so important to be rooted and established in love?*

If you are rooted & grounded in love, small or large troubles aren't going to move you

When asked the greatest commandment, Jesus actually lists two.

5. Read **Matthew 22:37–40**. *What are the two commandments? Which of the two is more difficult to obey? Why?*

Love the Lord & Love your neighbor.

Neighbor - you have to deal with them & their shortcomings all the time.

6. *Why do you think loving yourself is connected to loving your neighbor? Can you truly love your neighbor without loving yourself? Why or why not?* If you don't love yourself you are not able to truly reach out & love others, you are too busy trying to take care of yourself.

One of the most beautiful portraits of unconditional love is found in **1 Corinthians 13**. This is often described as the love chapter.

7. *Read **1 Corinthians 13:1–13** out loud. As you read this chapter, say your name every time the word* love *is used. When you're done, write your own definition of* love *in the space that follows.*

8. *How does unconditional love free people to be who they were created to be?*

Digging Deeper

Love is not just something that we experience, but at times it's something we choose. When we love, we choose patience, kindness, humility, and forgiveness. Read **Colossians 3:14**. What does it mean to you to "put on love"? How can you "put on love" each day in your home? Your workplace? Your community?

Ponder and Pray

The opening Scripture for this lesson comes from **Jeremiah 31:3**, "The LORD appeared to us in the past, saying: 'I have loved you with an everlasting love; I have drawn you with loving-kindness.'" In what specific ways has God revealed His loving-kindness to you? In what specific ways have you been able to reflect that loving-kindness to others?

The truth is, we are all designed not only to be loved unconditionally, but to love others unconditionally. As we discover the love that God has for each of us, we are better able to extend that love to others who need it most.

Bonus Activity

Take some time before God to ask Him if there are any people in your life whom you have been holding a grudge against in your heart. Ask God to reveal any stones of unforgiveness. On a blank sheet of paper, you may even want to write down the people's names. Ask God to forgive you for not forgiving them. Then ask God to bless the other people through prayer. If appropriate, you may even look for opportunities to reflect God's love to those people during the upcoming week by doing something thoughtful, kind, or generous for them.

Leader's Guide

Each chapter begins with an illustration and an icebreaker question intended to help the women in your group relax and join in the discussion. There isn't a "right" answer to any of these warm-up questions, so everyone can participate without fear of giving a wrong response. Try to include everyone in this part of the discussion to help everyone feel comfortable and become involved in the subject matter.

Eight discussion questions guide you through the content of each chapter. When you ask one of these questions, be sure to give your group plenty of time to think and don't be surprised if they grow silent temporarily. This is fairly common in discussion groups, and the leader who gives the group ample time to reflect will find they will open up and talk. To help you stay on track, this guide identifies questions intended to draw out opinions and provides information for questions aimed at more specific answers.

The highlighted box in the study states the main point of the chapter and corresponds to the **Focus** in the guide.

Digging Deeper is for those who want to do more thinking or digging in God's Word. This part is optional for discussion, but we hope you will want to go a little deeper in your study.

Ponder and Pray offers a great way to wrap up your study by reflecting on the opening Scripture. It's an opportunity for additional thoughts for reflection and prayer.

The Bonus Activity provides an opportunity to take an aspect of what you learned and place it into practice.

Just As You Are

Chapter 1: You Are God's Delight

> **Focus:** *The truth is that you are God's delight! You are of infinite worth and loved beyond measure.*

1. *This initial question is designed as an icebreaker question and hopefully provides an opportunity for group members to share some of the funny and even more ridiculous things all of us buy from time to time. Whether it's the promise of three easy payments of $19.95 or the scrubbing cleaner that guarantees you never have to scrub again, we've all purchased items that promise far more than they deliver.*

2. *There are many voices besides God that try to tell us who we are. Sometimes family members, friends, co-workers, bosses, and even people who don't love or appreciate us will try to define us. We may allow voices from the past—hurts, abuse, unresolved*

issues—to tell us who we are. God knows who we truly are and who we're created to be because He made us.

3. *God describes His saints as "the glorious ones in whom is all my delight." That means God doesn't just find some of His delight in you—He finds all of it. You are more celebrated than you can possibly imagine.*

4. *Delight and rejoicing are expressed in Proverbs 8:22–31. There is delight day after day. There is rejoicing in God's presence and in the world. There is delight in mankind.*

5. *Answers will vary. God delighted just as a craftsman delights in his work and takes pleasure from what he has created. If you've ever painted, written, designed, sculpted, or created something, then you've probably felt a surge of the joy and excitement that comes in the process of creating.*

6. *Answers will vary. You were a delight for God to create because you were formed in and out of His love. He took such time and care with every detail of your being. You are simply a delight to Him.*

7. *Answers will vary. In Zephaniah 3:17, we discover God is with us. He is mighty to save. He takes great delight in us. He quiets us with His love. He rejoices over us with singing. Participants may describe a variety of encounters with God's presence, provision, saving grace, peace, joy, and rest.*

8. *Answers will vary. Knowing that God delights in us naturally changes the way we see ourselves. It gives us a healthy perspective on who we are and who we're created to be. When we appreciate the beauty with which God has designed us, then we can better see it in other people.*

Chapter 2: You Are God's Handiwork

> **Focus:** *The truth is that you are God's handiwork.*
> *You are invited to be your true self.*

1. This initial question is designed as an icebreaker question. Like Anne, most women have at least one physical feature that they've struggled to accept about themselves. The point of this question is to highlight the fact that we can learn to accept and appreciate the way God has uniquely made each of us.

2. Some members of the group may not feel comfortable sharing, but those who do may highlight some crucial life stages when they discovered new things about themselves, including adolescence, marriage, motherhood, empty nest, retirement, etc. Encourage members to share how God was present during those times of discovery and transition.

3. Answers will vary. Few people will probably choose 1 or 10. Most will select something in the middle based on their personality, age, and stage in life. All answers are correct!

4.

Bible Passage	Who You Are In Christ
Philippians 3:20	I am a friend of Christ.
2 Corinthians 5:17	I have God's Spirit living within me.
John 1:12	I am a citizen of heaven.
John 15:15	I am a new creation.
1 Corinthians 3:16	I am a child of God.

5. *Answers will vary among participants.*

6. *Psalm 139:14 says, "I praise you because I am fearfully and wonderfully made; your works are wonderful, I know that full well."*

7. *Psalm 139:17–18 says, "How precious to me are your thoughts, O God! How vast is the sum of them! Were I to count them, they would outnumber the grains of sand. When I am awake, I am still with you." The psalmist recognized the great lengths God went to make him. He recognizes the detail and precision that went into his own design, and he worships God in response. When we discover that we are God's handiwork, we cannot help but worship God in response.*

8. *Answers will vary.*

Chapter 3: You Are Wonderfully Unique

Focus: *The truth is that you are wonderfully unique. God celebrates your uniqueness and wants to use you just as you are!*

1. *This is a fun, interactive icebreaker series of questions to allow the group members to enjoy both their similarities and differences.*

2. *While a few group members may be wearing the same color pattern, the odds are that no one's outfit matches exactly. We express our uniqueness in a variety of ways, including the clothes we wear, the way we decorate our homes, the foods we prefer, our hobbies, and the way we spend our time.*

3. *Answers will vary. While some people may only choose one personality trait, most people are a blend of at least two or more.*

4. *In many ways, Peter was the life of the party. He was always ready for an adventure and to dive in—but he was also distracted and not always dependable. Yet Jesus continued to use him and call him to a closer relationship with Himself. Through his time with Christ, Peter became a "rock" and an amazing evangelist.*

5. *Paul was a born leader. He followed the calling of God on his life with wholehearted abandon and inspired others to do the same. Even when he knew that his own death was near, he still remained faithful. He was extremely hardworking and committed to spreading the gospel as far as possible.*

6. *Abraham was rock solid. He was faithful, steady, and responsive to God's call on his life. When disagreement broke out over herdsmen, Abraham generously offered to give Lot the pick of the land because he knew the relationship was more important. When asked to sacrifice his son, Abraham responded in obedience. He knew the cost, but he also knew God's faithfulness.*

7. *Mary was a peacemaker. While her sister was busy making preparations, Mary was spending time with Jesus and showing her love for Him. But when Lazarus died, she was not the first to run after Jesus. She had resigned herself to the fact that Lazarus was dead. But once she was approached by Jesus, she openly shared her sense of loss with Him. She was steady and faithful.*

8. *Answers will vary.*

The Power of Being Yourself

Chapter 4: You Reflect God's Beautiful Design

> **Focus:** *The truth is that you inherently glorify God when you are yourself. God wants to spell something beautiful with your life—all you have to do is offer up the letters.*

1. This icebreaker question is meant to be a source of encouragement for everyone in the group as they get to know each other even better through this study.

2. This question is meant to highlight the fact that God uses us just as we are to bless and encourage others. At times, He does it even when we don't realize it!

3. Answers will vary, but Daniel is "spelling" or demonstrating faithfulness, conviction, and loyalty to God. He glorifies God in his faithfulness and choosing to honor God alone.

4. Answers will vary, but Nehemiah is "spelling" or demonstrating leadership, strength, and vision. When Sanballat the Horonite, Tobiah the Ammonite official, and Geshem the Arab try to discourage Nehemiah, he stands confident and resolved. Nehemiah is quick to acknowledge God as the One who will give success.

5. *Answers will vary, but Joseph is "spelling" or demonstrating purity, strength, conviction, and wisdom in this passage as he refuses to have an affair with his boss's wife. By resisting temptation, Joseph honors God.*

6. *Answers will vary, but Lydia is "spelling" or demonstrating hospitality, kindness, and generosity in this passage as she opens her home to Paul and those in ministry. Through her hospitality, she honors God.*

7. *Answers will vary, but this should be a gentle time of sharing.*

8. *Answers will vary, and some group members may not be comfortable sharing. But allow those who want to read their prayer express their desires to God.*

Chapter 5: You Will Set Others Free to Be Themselves

Focus: *The truth is that when you are yourself, you set others free to be themselves. You become a source of encouragement and blessing to others in ways you can't even imagine!*

1. *Answers will vary for this icebreaker question, but responses should highlight the fact that God uses all of us—just as we are—to make an impact on the lives of others.*

2. *Answers will vary.*

3. *Answers will vary.*

4. Elizabeth faced the challenge of infertility. In biblical times, this was particularly challenging as the children were to care for their parents as they aged. In addition to the financial challenges, there was a social stigma often attached to infertility.

5. Zechariah encountered Gabriel, an angel of God. The angel told him that his wife was going to become pregnant. Shortly after, Elizabeth conceived despite her age. Zechariah was unable to speak until the child was born.

6. Mary encountered Gabriel, an angel of God. The angel told her that she was going to become pregnant when the Holy Spirit came upon her.

7. Answers will vary. Mary and Elizabeth were able to encourage each other through the various challenges they had faced and unusual miraculous events they had experienced. Through their friendship, they were able to know they were not alone in all that they were experiencing and God was doing in their lives.

8. Answers will vary.

Chapter 6: You Help Fulfill God's Greater Purpose

Focus: The truth is, everyone has a role to play in making an impact on the world around them. When we offer ourselves—our whole selves—to God, He can use us in ways we can't even imagine!

1. *This introductory question is designed to cause participants to reflect on the unique way that they're wired and the kinds of issues, situations, and lives in which they're meant to get involved.*

2. *God wired each of us to be sensitive to particular burdens because each of us is designed to be used by God in a different way. If everyone had the exact same burden, then many needs would go unmet.*

3. *Answers will vary, but participants may pray, volunteer, donate their time or money, or serve in some capacity to become a solution to the situation.*

4. *Daniel did not have any physical defect. He was handsome, a great student, well-informed, and qualified to serve in the king's palace. God gave Daniel knowledge and understanding of all kinds of literature and learning. Daniel could understand visions and dreams of all kinds.*

5. *The burden that Daniel felt on his heart was not to defile himself with the royal food and wine. At the end of the time of eating, Daniel (and his friends) looked healthier and better nourished than any of the young men who ate the royal food.*

6. *Daniel responded with wisdom and tact. He found out what was really going on. Then he asked his friends to support him in prayer.*

7. *King Nebuchadnezzar honored Daniel and acknowledged that his God was the true God.*

8. *Daniel never knew the full impact he had on countless lives—including our own—as his prophecies are still unfolding today.*

No one can know the full impact that we will have by simply being ourselves and responding to the needs in our world.

Knowing Yourself

Chapter 7: Aware of Your Triggers

> **Focus:** *The truth is that by being aware of your weaknesses and the triggers that cause you to sin, you can learn to guard yourself from sin and focus your time and energy on your strengths.*

1. *Answers will vary, but participants may struggle with a variety of sins that express themselves in our attitudes including pride, anger, and selfishness. Some participants may be prone to sexual sins, addictions, or gluttony.*

2. *Answers will vary. Sometimes stress, busyness, lack of personal time with God, and lack of sleep can magnify struggles with sin or areas of weakness.*

3. *Prayer is the first step to identifying triggers. Ask God to reveal any activities or patterns that magnify temptation in your life. Being aware of your triggers is a key step to avoiding sin. Ask God to give you strength to resist temptation and the wisdom to know how to flee temptation.*

4. *One of Samson's weaknesses was sexual temptation. He had a weakness for women.*

5. Samson gave in to this area of weakness. He flirted with his weakness and temptation.

6. Samson became worn down by Delilah pressing him for information. She continually sought to know the source of Samson's strength, and even though Samson knew she would use the information against him, he stayed with her and eventually gave in to her. Samson could have avoided giving in to his weakness by leaving Delilah.

7. By giving in to sin, Samson allowed himself to become a defeated man. He was blinded, bound, and beaten. He was stripped of his strength and position.

8. When we give in to temptation, sin gets the best of us. Like Samson, we are left "blinded, bound, and beaten." Sin causes us to settle for less than God's best. While there is forgiveness and redemption through Jesus, when we sin we cannot be all we are created to be.

Chapter 8: Playing to Your Strengths

Focus: The truth is that every person has a unique blend of experiences, talents, and gifts that are meant to be used to honor God and serve others. When you focus on these areas, then you begin playing to your strengths. The impact will be unimaginable!

1. For many people, something less than becoming or even negative can slip into the description.

2. Answers will vary, but people have a tendency to focus on their weaknesses for a variety of reasons. Pressures to perform and measure up, report cards, and scorecards often reveal their strengths and weaknesses. If someone receives an A or near-perfect score, they may think they need not do any more work or focus on this area. Yet, such energy and focus would most likely make the person even better and possibly exceptional.

3. Answers will vary, but many people tend to focus on their weaknesses rather than their strengths.

4. Bezalel was given the skill, ability, and knowledge in all kinds of crafts to make artistic designs for work in gold, silver, and bronze. He could cut and set stones, work with wood, and do all kinds of artistic craftsmanship. His talent and skill was crucial for building the tabernacle—a place where God would dwell.

5. Answers will vary, but God gives us each different gifts that we may give to one another. If we had every gift and talent, then we wouldn't need each other. We wouldn't be as dependent on one another or reflect the church—the gathering of followers of Jesus—in the way God designed.

6. Most people have tried something that they weren't naturally good at. While we can learn new things and constantly grow, it's generally easier to hone a talent or gift than work at something where there's no natural talent or gift.

7. *Answers will vary. When people play to their strengths, the gifts God has given them naturally shine.*

8. *Answers will vary, but participants should be encouraged to respond and take action to this question.*

Chapter 9: Your Greatest Strength, Your Greatest Weakness

> **Focus:** *The truth is that our strengths and weaknesses are often linked. No one can be great at everything. That's why recognizing the link between strengths and weaknesses can help you develop compassion and grace not only for yourself but others.*

1. *Answers will vary, but often those who have gifts in one area do not inherently have them in another. For example, if you're highly creative, you may not be as well organized as someone who is analytical.*

2. *When we recognize that some strengths come with inherent weaknesses, then we are better able to extend compassion and grace to ourselves and others. We can drop unrealistic or unhealthy expectations and embrace people right where they are.*

3. *Answers will vary, but often people will notice that their gifts and personality tend to complement each other.*

4. *Martha's strength is hospitality. She welcomed Jesus into her home. Mary's strength is relational. She took time to spend with Jesus. Martha's strength of hospitality got the best of her when she was so focused on serving food that she lost focus on the One she was truly serving. She grew frustrated and worried. Mary was so focused on spending time with Jesus, she didn't take time to check to see if Martha needed any help.*

5. *Jesus responded firmly but full of compassion. Jesus loved both women, but He didn't want to see their strengths or weaknesses get the best of them. He reminded Martha that she had allowed the worry and frustration to get to her and assured Mary that she was doing what she was supposed to do. The passage reveals that at times our strengths and weaknesses will get the best of us, but Jesus is always there to help us lead balanced lives.*

6. *Answers will vary. Martha displayed her love for Jesus and strength of hospitality by going to meet Him. One of Martha's great strengths was her faith, which she displayed when she said she believed Jesus was the Son of God (v. 27). While Martha's angst regarding hospitality was clearly displayed in Luke 10:38–42, in this passage we see her hospitality as a great strength.*

7. *Answers will vary. While we will never know for sure her reasoning, Mary stayed home rather than go out and meet Jesus. When she was summoned, Mary displayed her love for Jesus by coming quickly when she was summoned. One of her strengths was expressiveness as she fell at Jesus' feet in tears. When Jesus saw Mary, He was deeply moved.*

8. *Answers will vary.*

The Fruit of Being Yourself

Chapter 10: Developing God-Esteem

> **Focus:** *The truth is, all of us have tremendous worth, but our value is not in what others think, but in what God thinks. God invites us to find our esteem in Him and live our lives for an audience of One.*

1. *God-esteem is better because God values and treasures us more than anyone else possibly can. While other people's opinions and thoughts of us may shift and change, God is steady in His love and commitment to us. In fact, God loves us so much that He sent His only Son to die for us. Our esteem will never be as high, solid, or consistent as when we find it in God.*

2. *All of us have areas where we're susceptible to finding our value and worth in someting other than God. We may want to be known as beautiful, intelligent, hardworking, or efficient, among other things. As a result, we find ourselves susceptible to flattery. And while others may see those things in us, their opinions may change. But God's opinion of us never changes. He finds value and worth in us that others will never be able to see.*

3. *Answers may vary, but living for an "audience of One" means finding our value, worth, and foundation in God. We no longer perform for everyone else, but we find our value and strength in God.*

4. First Samuel 15:29: Because God is not fickle. He does not lie or change His mind. Psalm 119:89–90: Because God's Word is eternal and He is faithful. Isaiah 46:4: Because He is the One who promises to sustain us, carry us, and rescue us all the days of our lives. Isaiah 54:10: Because God's love is unfailing. He has compassion on us.

5. We may be tempted to store up the approval or accolades of others. We may be tempted to store up awards, raises, job titles, or accomplishments. We may be tempted to store up compliments or what people think of us in our hearts. We should seek to store up the fruits of the Spirit in our hearts, including love, joy, peace, patience, and self-control.

6. Answers will vary, but it means that whatever we value as a treasure is a reflection of our hearts and what's truly important to us.

7. Answers will vary. We may find our treasure in our work, home, and families. While these are all good things, it's important to remember that our true treasure is God. He is the source of our strength to serve and love others.

8. Answers will vary.

Chapter 11: Radiating the Joy-Filled Life

Focus: The truth is that you are designed to radiate God's joy. As you grow in your relationship with God and worship, you can't help but radiate joy.

1. *Happiness is based on circumstance and is largely external, whereas joy is more dependent on inward character and faith no matter what happens. Happiness is largely dependent on what happens, whereas joy is dependent on who lives within us.*

2. *Answers will vary.*

3. *Answers will vary. Worry, anxiety, doubt, and fear often steal our joy.*

4. *This is the kind of joy that no one can take away.*

5. *The disciples were afraid and behind locked doors when Jesus came and stood among them. He said, "Peace be with you!" and showed the disciples His scars. This passage reveals that the disciples were overjoyed when they saw Jesus. It's interesting to note that the cause of their joy was not in a change of circumstance, but rather from just seeing Jesus.*

6. *God offers us the joy of His presence, and He offers us eternal pleasures—joy that lasts forever.*

7. *Psalm 33:21: "In him our hearts rejoice, for we trust in his holy name." Psalm 63:5: "My soul will be satisfied as with the richest of foods; with singing lips my mouth will praise you." Psalm 64:10: "Let the righteous rejoice in the LORD and take refuge in him; let all the upright in heart praise him!" Psalm 97:12: "Rejoice in the LORD, you who are righteous, and praise his holy name."*

8. *Answers will vary.*

Chapter 12: Loving Others Unconditionally

> **Focus:** *The truth is, we are all designed not only to be loved unconditionally, but to love others unconditionally. As we discover the love that God has for each of us, we are better able to extend that love to others who need it most.*

1. *Answers will vary. Participants may remember moments from childhood, adolescence, school, or church communities. They may recall certain individuals—a parent, teacher, coach, minister, or other person—who loved them unconditionally. Often, when we love others unconditionally, it sets us free to be our true selves. We no longer have to hold back in a relationship. We are encouraged to be ourselves and love others.*

2. *Answers will vary. Encourage participants to share stories from their past and present.*

3. *The distinguishing mark of believers is that they love one another.*

4. *Love is meant to be the foundation of who we are and who we're created to be. When we are rooted in the love of God, it transforms our actions, attitudes, and responses to be more like Christ.*

5. *Love the Lord your God with all your heart and with all your soul and with all your mind and love your neighbor as yourself. Answers will vary as to which is more difficult to obey.*

6. *Answers will vary, but it's hard to love others when we don't love ourselves. If you're hard on yourself, there's a natural tendency to be hard on other people. If you're critical of yourself, there's a natural tendency to be critical of other people. As we learn to love ourselves, complete with our imperfections, then we are free to love others.*

7. *Answers will vary.*

8. *Unconditional love accepts, encourages, and challenges. In many ways, it does everything that 1 Corinthians 13 describes.*

About the Author

Margaret Feinberg is an author and speaker who offers a refreshing perspective on faith and the Bible. She has written more than a dozen books including *The Organic God* and *God Whispers*. She also wrote the Women of Faith Bible Study *Overcoming Fear*. Margaret is a popular speaker at women's events, luncheons, and retreats as well as national conferences including Catalyst, LeadNow, Fusion, and the National Pastor's Conference.

She lives in Lakewood, Colorado, in the shadow of the Rockies with her 6'8" husband, Leif. When she's not writing and traveling, she loves hiking, shopping, blogging, laughing, and drinking skinny vanilla lattes with her girlfriends. But some of her best days are spent communicating with her readers.

So if you want to put a smile on her face, go ahead and write her!

Margaret@margaretfeinberg.com

www.margaretfeinberg.com

www.margaretfeinberg.blogspot.com

Tag her on Facebook or follow her on twitter

www.twitter.com/mafeinberg

Additional Resources

What Shall We Study Next?

Women of Faith® has numerous study guides out right now
that will draw you closer to God.

Living Above Worry and Stress

*Consider the lilies, how they grow: they neither toil
nor spin; and yet I say to you, even Solomon in all
his glory was not arrayed like one of these. If then
God so clothes the grass, which today is in the field
and tomorrow is thrown into the oven, how much
more will He clothe you, O you of little faith?*

LUKE 12:27–28, NKJV

The words echo back to us from years gone by. We first learned it in a Vacation Bible School one summer or from a dear Sunday school teacher—the voice of Jesus calling us to consider the lilies. The lesson was a simple one: don't worry. If God would give the flowers such pretty petals, dressing them more grandly than wealthy King Solomon could manage, He will provide for our needs too.

Unfortunately, the call to consider the lilies is left on a dusty shelf somewhere. It's probably right next to the old plea to stop and smell the roses. We're too busy for stopping. We're too rushed for consideration. Our "to do" lists are long. Our day timers are booked. Our time is money. We can't keep up.

We are busy people. We have responsibilities at work. We have responsibilities at home. We have responsibilities at church. We have responsibilities at school. We have responsibilities within our communities. We care for the needs of our parents, our husbands, our children, our siblings, our employers, our closest friends. Most days, it is more than we can handle. Our hearts are overwhelmed. We are stressed out. We are worried. We dread tomorrow.

In the midst of all this everyday turmoil, our hearts long for a place of peace. We know God has promised us rest. We know He says we don't have to worry about tomorrow. He promised to calm our fears. Yet we barely have time to whisper a prayer, let alone study our Bibles. If you have been struggling, come. Let's take a little time to explore the Scriptures, and find some practical guidelines for laying aside our fears, our worry, and even our stress. You really can discover a place of peace.

Living in Jesus

Those who become Christians become new persons.
They are not the same anymore, for the old life is
gone. A new life has begun!

2 CORINTHIANS 5:17, NLT

Have you ever read books just to escape the never-ending dullness of everyday life? Through the chapters of some paperback, we experience the shadows of an existence that seems more interesting, more exciting, more appealing than what our own day has to offer. Damsels find unfailing love, sleuths seek out elusive clues, strangers form unlikely alliances, adventurers cross unfamiliar terrains, and they all live happily ever after. In comparison, we feel boring, listless, and wistful.

Little do we realize that as believers, we have been ushered into a life that rivals the plot of any mere story! We have become leading ladies in a thrilling tale of epic proportions. There's something for everyone: combat, romance, intrigue, drama, rescue, duplicity, character development, action, adventure, complex subplots, moral dilemmas, sacrifice, tear jerking, subtle humor, slapstick, subterfuge, betrayal, showdowns, discovery, unexpected twists, irony, paradise, and a happy ending.

The Christian life is vibrant, mysterious, and beautiful. In a word— sensational! Open your eyes to the wonder of a life knit with the divine. Jesus has called you, chosen you, changed you. Your life is caught up with His, transformed into something altogether new. Jesus is your intimate friend—familiar, inseparable, precious. He has called you His beloved, and made you fantastic promises. Your life is a never-ending story that will continue to unfold throughout eternity.

All because of what you are *in Him.*

Adventurous Prayer: Talking with God

Prayer is reaching out to touch Someone—namely,
your Creator. In the process, He touches you.

BARBARA JOHNSON

What's the big deal about prayer? We know we should all do it more often, take it more seriously, and give it more time—but we don't. Does that mean that prayer is optional? After all, some of the other spiritual disciplines seem pretty outdated, like fasting and solitude. Who has time for that? That kind of stuff is for monks, nuns, and pastors. We've gotten along okay without it.

So, does prayer fit into the *non*-essentials of the Christian walk? Prayer must be that "in case of emergency" last-resort kind of spiritual tool. Right?

Shame on you!

Prayer isn't some kind of requirement for believers. It is a privilege! You have the ear of the Divine. Prayer is our path to the adventure of building a relationship with our Savior.

God knows what's going on in your life. The Creator of all that is stoops to hear the lisping of toddlers. The Sustainer of every living thing hears the groans and sighs of the aging. He is aware of every thought, every choice, every move you make—but He is waiting for you to turn to Him and tell Him about it.

God listens to you. He will answer you.

THE COMPLETE WOMEN OF FAITH®
STUDY GUIDE SERIES

OVERCOMING FEAR

UNDERSTANDING PURPOSE

RECEIVING GOD'S GOODNESS

RECEIVING GOD'S LOVE

CONTAGIOUS JOY

A LIFE OF WORSHIP

DISCOVERING GOD'S WILL FOR YOUR LIFE

CULTIVATING CONTENTMENT

EXPERIENCING SPIRITUAL INTIMACY

GIVING GOD YOUR ALL

LIVING ABOVE WORRY AND STRESS

ENCOURAGING ONE ANOTHER

AMAZING FREEDOM

MANAGING YOUR MOODS

LIVING IN JESUS

KNOWING GOD'S WORD

LIVING A LIFE OF BALANCE

ADVENTUROUS PRAYER

To find these and other inspirational products visit your local Christian retailer.

WOMEN OF FAITH

THOMAS NELSON
Since 1798

WOMEN OF FAITH
DEVOTIONAL JOURNAL

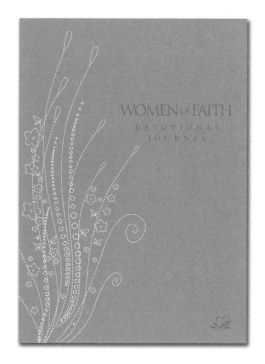

*T*he *Women of Faith Devotional Journal*
speaks directly to the subject of God's infinite grace. Filled with
stirring quotes and uplifting Scripture, this journal is the ideal
addition to any devotional time.

- Scripture verses highlight wisdom for daily life

- Your favorite Women of Faith speakers' enlightening
  thoughts on grace

- Plenty of writing space to record dreams, hopes,
  and personal reflections

WOMEN OF FAITH

THOMAS NELSON
Since 1798